Straight Talk About...
CHILD ABUSE

Sydney Newton
and Julie Gerrits

Crabtree Publishing Company
www.crabtreebooks.com

Straight Talk About...

Developed and produced by: Plan B Book Packagers

Editorial director: Ellen Rodger

Art director: Rosie Gowsell-Pattison

Fictional Introductions: Rachel Eagen

Editor: Molly Aloian

Project coordinator: Kathy Middleton

Production coordinator: Margaret Amy Salter

Prepress technician: Margaret Amy Salter

Consultant: Susan Rodger, PhD., C. Psych., Psychologist and Professor Faculty of Education, The University of Western Ontario

Photographs:
Title page: EJ White/Shutterstock Inc.; p.4: Justin Paget/Shutterstock Inc.; p. 6: Serhiy Kyrychenko/Shutterstock Inc.; p. 9: Suzanne Tucker/Shutterstock Inc.; p. 10: Silver-John/Shutterstock Inc.; p. 11: Zurijeta/Shutterstock Inc.; p. 12: J. Gould/iStockPhoto.com; p. 14: Larisa Lofitskaya/Shutterstock Inc.; p. 15: EJ White/Shutterstock Inc.; p. 16: Aleksei Potov/Shutterstock Inc.; p. 18: Margot Petrowski/Shutterstock Inc.; p. 19: Karuka/Shutterstock Inc.; p. 20: Golden Pixels LLC/Shutterstock Inc.; p. 21: MotoEd /iStockPhoto.com; p. 22: (left) @erics/Shutterstock Inc., (right) Rob Byron/Shutterstock Inc.; p. 23: Justin Paget/Shutterstock Inc.; p. 24: Gina Sanders/Shutterstock Inc.; p. 26: IB/iStockPhoto.com; p. 27: Nir Levy/Shutterstock Inc.; p. 28: Track 5/iStockPhoto.com; p. 29: Elena Rostunova/Shutterstock Inc.; p. 30: Julia Pivovarova/Shutterstock Inc.; p. 31: Creatista/Shutterstock Inc.; p. 33: Zurijeta/Shutterstock Inc.; p. 34: Dimitris_K./Shutterstock Inc.; p. 35: Justin Paget/Shutterstock Inc.; p. 36: Nina Malyna/Shutterstock Inc.; p. 38: (left) Blazej Maksym/Shutterstock Inc., ZouZou/Shutterstock Inc.; p. 39: Light Poet/Shutterstock Inc.; p. 40: Lisa F. Young/Shutterstock Inc.

Library and Archives Canada Cataloguing in Publication

Newton, Sydney
    Child abuse / Sydney Newton and Julie Gerrits.

(Straight talk about--)
Includes index.
Issued also in an electronic format.
ISBN 978-0-7787-2127-7 (bound).--ISBN 978-0-7787-2134-5 (pbk.)

    1. Child abuse--Juvenile literature. I. Gerrits, Julie II. Title.
III. Series: Straight talk about-- (St. Catharines, Ont.)

HV6626.5.N49 2010   j362.76   C2010-903370-1

Library of Congress Cataloging-in-Publication Data

Newton, Sydney.
    Child abuse / Sydney Newton and Julie Gerrits.
        p. cm. -- (Straight talk about--)
    Includes index.
    ISBN 978-0-7787-2134-5 (pbk. : alk. paper) --
    ISBN 978-0-7787-2127-7 (reinforced library binding : alk. paper)
    -- ISBN 978-1-4271-9540-1 (electronic (pdf))
    1. Child abuse--Juvenile literature. I. Gerrits, Julie. II. Title.
III. Series.

HV6626.5.N495 2011
362.76--dc22
                                                    2010019912

Crabtree Publishing Company

www.crabtreebooks.com   1-800-387-7650

Printed in China/082010/AP20100512

Published in Canada
Crabtree Publishing
616 Welland Ave.
St. Catharines, ON
L2M 5V6

Published in the United States
Crabtree Publishing
PMB 59051
350 Fifth Avenue, 59th Floor
New York, NY 10118

Published in the United Kingdom
Crabtree Publishing
Maritime House
Basin Road North, Hove
BN41 1WR

Published in Australia
Crabtree Publishing
386 Mt. Alexander Rd.
Ascot Vale (Melbourne)
VIC 3032

CONTENTS

Kelly walked home from school with the feeling in her chest. That heavy feeling. There'd been empty bottles in the kitchen this morning, and Dad had slept on the couch again.

Things hadn't been the same since Dad got fired. He'd always been scary when he got mad, but lately, he was always mad.

She opened the door with her house key. It was empty and dark inside. She tiptoed to the kitchen to make a snack.

"What're you doing?" Dad stared at her from a kitchen chair. His eyes were red and he looked very tired.

"I'm just—"

"You're just nothing. Go play."

"Mom lets me have a snack after school."

"I'm not Mommy. And I said get out of here."

Kelly climbed the stairs with tears in her eyes. She shut the door to her room and sat on the floor. "Stupid," she says to herself. "I'm so stupid." Downstairs, she heard a cupboard slam and the sound of her dad swearing.

Introduction
Abuse of Trust

Kelly doesn't know that what's happening to her is wrong. She knows it feels bad, but she doesn't know that she needs help to make it stop. Like many young people who are abused, she blames herself for her dad's behavior, and she thinks that if she is really good, she can make it stop.

Child abuse can mean a lot of different things. It means hurting a child either with hands or with words, or not making sure the child goes to school, has enough food to eat, or a safe place to sleep. Most of the time the abuser is someone the child should be able to trust and depend on, such as a parent, relative, babysitter, teacher, or coach.

In this book, you will learn more about child abuse and why it's wrong. You will also learn how to find the right place to go and talk to someone if you or a friend is being abused, or if you have more questions about child abuse.

"Abuse is something that cannot always be seen. Abuse hurts people on the inside and outside, and the pain feels worse when it is kept a secret."
Vanessa, child and family therapist.

Chapter 1
What Is Child Abuse?

All children have the right to feel safe and be free from harm regardless of their age, **gender**, race, or background. This is a basic **human right**. In spite of this, not everyone lives in an environment where they feel cared for and safe. There are many children, adolescents, and teens just like you who are being hurt—abused by people they love and depend upon. You may be friends with someone who is being abused now and not even know it. Or you may be **experiencing** abuse yourself and not know what to do about it.

What Is Child Abuse?

Child abuse happens when an adult a child trusts or depends on hurts, mistreats, or does not care for them. Child abuse is against the law. A child can be abused by a parent, **sibling**, coach, or teacher, as well as someone they are less close to, such as a friend's parent. Adults who are in a position of trust should always have a child's best interest at heart, and should teach them, protect them, and encourage them to do well. An adult who is abusing a child is **violating** the child's trust. They are putting themselves first, often by taking their frustrations out on a child, or using power to control them.

Where Does Abuse Happen?

Abuse can occur anywhere, including your home, a friend's house, or at school. Any child can be a victim of abuse, regardless of age, race, gender, or family income. There are different forms of abuse, including physical abuse, emotional or psychological abuse, sexual abuse, and neglect. All forms of abuse are against the law and harmful to children, regardless of whether the harm is caused by fists, words, or touch.

Hurtful and Harmful

Psychologists call all forms of child abuse child maltreatment. Maltreatment means to treat someone cruelly or with **coercion** or violence. Physical abuse happens when an adult or someone in a position of power harms a child's body. An adult is abusing you if he or she is hitting or kicking you when they are mad. Emotional abuse, or what is often called inside hurting, occurs when an adult says hurtful things that make you feel bad about yourself or if the adult acts in a **manipulative** way. If a teacher tells your friend they are "stupid" or a "waste of space," it is emotional abuse. Emotional abuse also includes hearing or seeing someone else, such as a parent, being abused. Sexual abuse occurs when an adult, older adolescent, or teen touches a child in places that are private, such as the genitals, buttocks, or breasts. Neglect is another form of abuse that happens when an adult does not take proper care of a child. A friend who is experiencing neglect may have parents who do not feed them during the day or who leave them with caregivers who are not trustworthy. Although each type of abuse is different, one thing always remains the same—abuse is never a child's fault.

How Common Is Abuse?

Child abuse is a hidden problem. Experts think the instances of child abuse are much higher than reported. This sometimes happens because most abuse is investigated by the police or child welfare authorities, who require a complaint to get involved. Children who are being abused may be too scared or embarrassed to tell anyone what is happening for fear they or their abusers will get into trouble, or that they won't be believed. Some never tell anyone. Each year, there are over 1.8 million child abuse investigations in the United States alone.

Rough treatment may seem so normal that kids might not understand that what is happening to them is abuse.

Who Is at Risk?

Although abuse can happen to anyone, some things make some children more at risk. These include:

- Living in a home where violence is happening between two parents.

- Living in a home where a parent or adult caregiver is addicted to drugs or alcohol.

- Living in a home where a parent or adult caregiver has a mental health condition that they are not receiving treatment or support for.

- Living in a home where parents or adult caregivers are under a great deal of stress.

Why Does It Happen?

Child abuse has no single cause. There are many things that contribute to abuse. Abuse is often about power and control. Abusers have the power and are able to use it to control children, adolescents, and teenagers. It is an adult's job to ensure that children in their care are safe and free from harm. Sometimes adults are not able or willing to care for children because of **addictions** or stresses in their lives. This is not a child's fault, but is a result of an adult situation a child has little control over. Abuse also happens when an adult oversteps the boundaries of discipline—taking punishment and correction of children too far.

Fists should never be used to solve problems.

Effects of Abuse

Abuse influences how children, adolescents, and teens think, feel, and act. It can affect someone immediately, such as while the abuse is occurring. It can also affect someone long after the abuse has ended, in adulthood. Someone who is being abused may feel embarrassed, ashamed, or as if the abuse is their fault. As a result, they may keep the abuse to themselves, which can cause them to feel as if they are all alone. If you are being abused, you may also feel confused about why it is happening, and you may want to protect the person who is hurting you. A boy who is being abused by his father, for example, may be confused about what to do because he knows that what is happening is wrong, but loves his dad and does not want him to get into trouble.

Abuse may be confusing for children, who may think they deserve to be hurt or mistreated.

"I am so confused and do not know how to fix it. One day my dad is so nice to me and my brother, but the next day he is angry and hurts us. I don't know what I am doing to make him nice one day, and hit me the next."
Jacob, aged 10.

Chapter 2
Physical Abuse

A black eye or bloody lip are what people imagine when they think of physical abuse. But physical abuse is not just deliberate beatings and assaults. It can be severe discipline or physical punishment, as well.

Sticks, Stones, and Broken Bones

Physical abuse is the most visual or obvious type of abuse. It involves situations where an adult hurts or injures a child's body. The abuse may be **intentional**, such as when a parent or caregiver hits a child while angry, or **unintentional**, such as when a parent is angry and throws a chair that accidentally hits a child. Some examples of physical abuse include hitting, kicking, or choking a child, pushing a child down the stairs, hitting a child with an object such as a belt or shoe, burning a child with a cigarette, or purposefully putting a child in a situation where they are likely to be hurt. Physical punishment does not have to leave a mark or visible scars to be abuse.

"How could I tell anyone what was happening to me if I didn't trust them? I never knew what to say or how to say it. I was scared that if they knew they would take me away and make me live with people I didn't know. Or that they would tell my mom and things would get worse."
Thomasina, aged 15.

Causing Harm

Physical abuse is the second most commonly reported type of abuse, after neglect. Physical abuse not only causes harm to a child's body in the form of cuts, bruises, and broken bones, it also causes emotional harm. Children who are physically abused are more at risk for developing **emotional disorders** such as **anxiety**, **depression**, and post-traumatic stress disorder (PTSD) because of their early experiences with violence. They may also have trouble forming trusting relationships and even trusting their own judgments and inner voice. Although the risk for these things is higher for those who have been abused, many survivors of abuse are strong, caring people. Abuse does not have to define who a person is and how they behave throughout their lives.

Fear, Control, and Power

Children can become victims of physical abuse at any age, including when they are infants. When it comes to those who physically abuse children, **perpetrators** are not limited to any specific gender, age, race, or income level. Most don't have anything in common except a belief in power and force. Abusers use fear to control their victims. Some don't understand or accept that this is wrong. They may be influenced by their own past experiences or by the society or culture they live in that views violence as normal. This can make it even more difficult for their victims who may start to believe their maltreatment is normal and acceptable—even if it frightens and hurts them.

Children might not have the words to say that they are being abused. Sometimes they react to abuse with anger or fear.

Abuse vs. Discipline

You may have heard your grandparents describe getting their "hide tanned" or getting a "whuppin" from their parents for misbehaving as a child. The hurt and **humiliation** obviously wasn't something they forgot. Years ago, severe forms of discipline such as hitting with belts and **switches** was considered acceptable. Most schools even had **corporal punishment** such as hand slapping and strappings for children who disobeyed rules. Today, we know this form of punishment is not effective and is in fact hurtful and abusive. Sometimes abuse is explained as discipline "gone too far." Physical discipline that humiliates and hurts a child or leaves visible marks is abuse. It makes a child feel worthless and fearful. Discipline is intended to guide, direct, or correct behavior. It should be clear, predictable, and consistent and should not be given when a parent or caregiver is very angry and might not be able to control themselves.

Disciplining with weapons, such as belts or spoons is physical abuse.

Physical Abuse Warning Signs

There are some warning signs that a child may be experiencing physical abuse. However, it is important to note that these are warning signs, not proof positive that abuse is occurring. You can always ask a child is they are being abused, but they may not trust you or may be too frightened to tell the truth. Some warning signs are listed below:

- Unexplained bruises, cuts, or marks on a child's body

- A child who is being abused may become shy or uncomfortable when asked about their bruises, and may change their story about how they got the mark. In addition, they may wear clothing that covers up their marks so that other people will not notice.

- Some children appear "jumpy," nervous, or shy when they hear a loud noise, or when someone tries to touch them.

- A child may be nervous or shy when someone is angry because they are used to being hurt by other adults when they are angry.

- Unreasonable or unexplained fear of leaving a safe place or not wanting to go home

- A child frequently misses days at school or special events, or has frequent nightmares.

- Unexplained anger or aggression towards schoolmates or other children

"My grandma took care of us but treated me different than my younger brothers. Sometimes she called me names and they always got more things and better clothes. I didn't get why she didn't like me. I thought I could make her love me some day. It really hurt."
Tanya, aged 17.

Chapter 3
Emotional Abuse

Emotional abuse is an inside-hurting form of abuse that creates deep scars to a person's sense of self-worth. It can be subtle, such as constant suggestions that a child isn't wanted or worthy of love. It can also be blatant, such as yelling or screaming or name calling.

How Do You Define It?

There is no universally accepted definition of emotional abuse, which makes it difficult to identify and easy to deny. Emotional abuse happens when someone speaks or expresses to a child that they are worthless, useless, unimportant, imperfect, or unloved. There is the old belief that "words don't hurt," which is not true. Hurtful words cause just as much, if not more, emotional damage to a child as physical abuse. Emotional abuse takes on many forms including rejecting, degrading, terrorizing, **isolating**, **exploiting**, and denying attention or love. All types of emotional abuse involve adult caregivers using power to control a child, adolescent, or teen who depends on them.

Threatening Behavior

Emotional abuse can be aggressive and include such things as name calling or threats, blaming, accusing, or ordering. If a parent, caregiver, coach, or teacher calls you an idiot and tells you that you are the cause of all their problems, it is emotionally abusive. Other examples of emotional abuse include threatening with violence, humiliation, refusing to hug or kiss a child, and telling a child they are no-good or will not go anywhere in life.

Occasional teasing is normal in family relationships. It becomes abusive if it is used as a way to control or humiliate someone.

What About Teasing?

Emotional abuse is so common that you may wonder whether certain things that occur in your home or in social situations would be considered emotional abuse. It is common in many families for members to tease or bug each other. Some of this behavior is normal and not abusive, such as an older brother occasionally calling his little brother a name. The differences between abusive and non-abusive behavior are slight at times. When jokes at people's expense occur frequently, causing them to feel bad about themselves, and are used as a way to exert power and control, it is emotional abuse.

Emotional abuse can be difficult to recognize in society, as there are many situations where this type of behavior is considered normal or "just the way it is." It can be easy to overstep the boundaries between teasing and instruction to taunting and abuse. Organized sports is one area where ridicule, humiliation, and abuse is often accepted and sometimes rewarded. Coaches may need to raise their voices to be heard on noisy basketball courts, football fields, or hockey arenas. They don't need to curse and belittle their players. A coach who screams in red-faced fury has lost control and is abusing his or her authority.

Coaches don't need to threaten or abuse to get the best out of players.

Lasting Effects

When a parent or caregiver makes negative comparisons between children, or rejects a child as a form of punishment, these too are forms of emotional abuse. Emotional abuse often has long-lasting effects. It can harm a child's ability to feel, share, and understand feelings, and can destroy their sense of self-worth or self-esteem. Self-esteem is a person's belief in their importance and abilities. People with low self-esteem have a hard time accepting that they have skills and abilities and are worthy of love and **affection**. As adults, they may form relationships with other abusive people or become abusive themselves in an attempt to assert power over other people to make themselves feel better.

It takes a lot of work to regain the self-esteem lost through constant abuse, but it can be done.

The Hurt Inside

Sometimes emotional abuse can be so **traumatic** that a child can have a hard time forming relationships with adults who care for them. Psychologists call this an **attachment disorder**. Attachment disorders can result in emotional or behavioral problems such anger or an inability to feel, share, and understand feelings. Kids who have been abused learn that the world is not a safe place and they can't trust adults to take care of them, so it is hard to form trusting relationships.

Emotional abuse can make children more anxious, constantly fearful, and even depressed. They may struggle with everyday life, and have a hard time eating, or getting out of bed. Often, children won't know what is wrong with them. They may have constant stomachaches or headaches from dealing with the pressure of abuse. When they are depressed, they may feel tired and have difficulty sleeping or concentrating. These feelings may continue for weeks or months. Children, teens, and adults can all suffer from depression.

Depression can make some people have suicidal thoughts.

"He touches me in places that do not feel right. It feels funny, weird, and scary because usually no one is around. I promised I would not tell, and he gave me gifts sometimes. I have kept this a secret for a long time because I do not want him to get into trouble. I have many confusing feelings."
Miranda, aged 11.

Chapter 4
Sexual Abuse

Child sexual abuse and exploitation are hidden and complicated forms of abuse. For many years, people did not want to talk about sexual abuse or admit that it happens. Avoiding discussions about sexual abuse or denying reports of sexual abuse makes victims feel **abandoned** and alone.

Both girls and boys at any age can be victims of sexual abuse. Sexual abuse occurs when a child is used for a sexual purpose, or is exposed to sexual behavior or activity. This includes sexual touching on their genitals, penis, vagina, anus, breasts, or other body parts. It also includes rape, oral sex, or other acts. Sexual abuse also occurs when a child is forced or invited to touch an adult's genitals. Sexual abuse does not always include bodily contact. Exposing children to sexual behavior or activity, such as watching others have sex or inviting or forcing them to watch pornography on the television or computer, is sexual abuse. Those who commit child sexual abuse often know or have close relationships with the children they abuse.

It's a Crime

The sexual abuse of children, like other forms of child abuse, is against the law. Sometimes people are charged, found guilty, and sent to jail for their crimes. Often, they continue hurting children because children are too afraid to tell anyone about their abuse for fear they won't be believed or that people will think it is their fault. Child sexual abuse is never the child's fault. Adults have all the power and responsibility. Nothing children do "makes" an adult abuse them. Adults who know about the sexual abuse of children, but choose to say or do nothing about it, can also be charged with a crime. It is their duty to protect children from harm.

Not Alone

Statistics show that about 25 percent of adult women and five to 15 percent of adult men were sexually abused as children. Their abusers tended mostly to be relatives, such as fathers, mothers, brothers, uncles, cousins, or friends of the family, such as neighbors, babysitters, priests, or ministers. People who are sexually attracted to and prey on children for sex are called pedophiles. Some pedophiles and abusers see nothing wrong with what they do, even when it hurts a child physically and mentally.

Sexual abusers prey on children of all ages.

Sexual Exploitation

Sexual exploitation includes situations where a child is sought out by an adult who wishes to use them for sexual activities. Examples include making a film of a child to be used in child pornography, speaking with a child on the Internet for sexual purposes, as well as making a child participate in sexual acts for money.

Children are sexually exploited both by people they know and by strangers. Sometimes children, adolescents, and teens are forced into having sex with strangers because they promise money or other things such as food or a place to stay. People who do these things are child abusers. Increasingly, sexual **predators** are using the Internet to lure children and teens into performing sexual acts. Some predators pose as same-age friends to fool children and teens into thinking they are interested in friendships and not in harming them.

Many predators are smart. They study children and target them by using language they understand.

Sexual Predators

Children, adolescents, and teens want to be liked by others. This makes them easy prey to abusers. Often, sexual abusers, or predators, will get to know children before they abuse them. They may shower them with attention to make them feel good, loved, special, and wanted. Psychologists call this grooming. A child who is being groomed by their teacher may be given gifts, special privileges at school, or higher grades. In response to this special treatment it is normal for a child to feel a special bond with the adult, which can make them confused when they are later asked or forced to participate in a sexual activity. It is normal for children to feel they "owe" it to the adult, or as if the adult would not do something to hurt them. But grooming is all about establishing power and control over a child.

Predators "groom" by giving special attention and gaining the trust of children.

Dealing with the Pain

Sexual abuse hurts in so many ways—physically, mentally, and socially. Many children experience overwhelming feelings of shame, making it even more difficult for them to tell anyone that they are being abused. Since most children are abused by someone they know, they may also feel like they must protect them from jail. Abusers also manipulate those they hurt. Some may threaten a child to prevent them from telling anyone.

Even long after the abuse, the pain remains. Children who experience sexual abuse are more likely to suffer from anxiety, depression, and PTSD. These are medical conditions or disorders that arise from the trauma of abuse. PTSD is a response to severe trauma where a person's safety has been threatened. People with PTSD have trouble concentrating, sleeping, and sometimes controlling anger. Some may relive the trauma over and over again or feel detached from everyday experiences.

PTSD can make people feel they are reliving their trauma over and over again, even years after their experience.

"The only way I could deal with my abuse was to deny it. I denied that it had any impact on my life but it did. I pretended that I was strong and able to handle this by myself, but I was angry and my anger came out and affected my relationships with everyone in my life."
Andrew, adult survivor of child sexual abuse.

Warning Signs

There are some warning signs that a child may be experiencing sexual abuse. However, like other types of abuse, they are not proof that sexual abuse is occurring. Signs include:

- Inappropriate knowledge of sex for their age

- Children who have been exposed to a lot of sexual material may repeat or imitate noises or movements they have seen in person, on DVDs, or the Internet.

- A sexually transmitted infection (STI) at a young age is another warning sign.

- Other warning signs include changes in behavior and strong fears of going to visit a certain person or place.

Missing Boundaries

Children who have been sexually abused may have difficulty with **boundaries** or knowing how to act with other children. They may sometimes touch other children in ways that are inappropriate or not safe because they have learned to interact with others in ways their abusers taught them. Boundaries keep us safe, so we know what is allowed and what is not okay. When boundaries are violated through sexual abuse, things can get blurry and confused.

Responses to Abuse

Many children who have been abused have difficulties concentrating in school and trouble sleeping. They are less likely to feel safe, have a hard time controlling their emotions, and are more likely to think bad things about themselves. When children feel unsafe and have a hard time concentrating, they may also have difficulties in school or get poor grades. In addition, those who have experienced abuse are more likely to have difficulties with later relationships, including trusting and connecting with others. Some may even turn to coping mechanisms such as **self-injury** and drug or alcohol abuse to numb the pain.

Children who have been abused sometimes turn to drugs to deal with their pain and anger.

"I came home every day after school to my parents
sleeping on the couch. They always seemed too
sleepy to help me at night. I always made dinner or
whatever, and put my sister to bed. I knew it was not
normal. My friends got bedtime stories, but not me."
Emily, aged 15.

Chapter 5
Neglect

Child neglect is the most reported form of child abuse. It is often easy to see but hard to change. An adult may be neglecting a child and not even realize that they are committing child abuse.

Neglect occurs when a caregiver does not provide proper care for a child who relies on them. Proper care means ensuring children have adequate food, supervision, clothing, housing, education, and medical care. Sometimes, neglect is a matter of money. When parents or caregivers are poor, they sometimes cannot afford to feed or clothe their children. Neglected children are also less likely to be taken to the doctor or hospital for medical treatment.

A child who is neglected may not be fed regularly or get help with daily tasks that are required for them to be healthy physically and mentally. For example, if a parent spends much of their time out with their friends or on the computer and never feeds, gives affection, or bathes their child, then that child is neglected.

All Too Common

Neglect is a common form of abuse. Over 540,000 children were reported neglected in the last census year. Children who experience neglect are more likely to have health problems, be placed in dangerous situations, or experience depression and low self-esteem.

The factors that can place caregivers at risk for committing neglect are similar to other types of abuse. They suffer high levels of stress, often from coping with **poverty**, and are more likely to have untreated mental health conditions, as well as drug and alcohol addictions. Addictions make it difficult for a parent or caregiver to function normally since addicts spend most of their time and money trying to get and stay high or drunk. Parents or caregivers with mental health problems are often not capable of giving their children the level of care and attention they need. They may not intend to cause harm to their children, but their disease prevents them from doing what is best.

Neglect is more common in families coping with poverty and substance abuse.

Warning Signs of Neglect

There are a number of possible warning signs that a child may be experiencing neglect. A child who appears unhealthy, tired, and is frequently hungry or dirty may be neglected. In extreme cases a child may die due to starvation or not being taken to a doctor when they were very sick. Other warning signs include when a child does not want to go home, always comes to school without a lunch, or when a child talks about how they are home alone a lot and often have to make their own dinner.

If you are hungry all the time, you can't concentrate on school tasks, so your marks suffer. Children who are underfed are sick more often because their bodies are not nourished enough to fight off common diseases. Children who are left alone and unsupervised also have a greater chance of injury or death from accidents.

Neglect often leaves children to cope with adult problems and forces them to take on adult roles.

Chapter 6
Seeking Help

If you are being abused by someone you love or respect, it can be a terrible and scary thing to deal with. Abuse can make you feel like the loneliest person in the world. You may believe that you don't deserve better, that there is no hope for you, or that you caused the abuse.

A child is never to blame for abuse, and is never the only one who has experienced abuse. Kids often keep abuse a secret for some time before sharing their story with someone. Keeping abuse a secret can make it worse. It protects the abuser and makes the abused feel more alone.

Some secrets are just not meant to be kept.

Reaching Out

It is difficult to stop abuse on your own. You will need help from others to get you out of the abusive situation. Try not to feel ashamed or guilty about asking for help. You may have a horrible feeling in the pit of your stomach thinking about telling someone what is happening to you. This is natural. It is normal to feel worried, scared, or unsure. It takes a lot of courage to reach out. You can practice telling someone in a mirror or in a quiet place. It can sometimes help to know what you want to say ahead of time.

"I told my teacher that my grandpa was hurting me. I was so scared and my tummy hurt when I shared my secret. She listened to me and believed me."
Patrick, aged 11

There is help out there. It takes a lot of courage to ask for it.

Who Can You Trust?

If you tell a trusted adult that you are being abused, they might call the police or child-welfare authorities to report it. In some places, and for some adults, they are required by law to tell the authorities. If this happens, police and child-welfare workers will talk to you about what will happen next. Their first and most important responsibility is to keep children safe. If you are not sure who you can trust, you can call a helpline. The counselor on the line can help you sort through your feelings and give you direction or advice on what to do next. You can find helplines in a phonebook or try the numbers listed on page 47 of this book.

Helping a Friend

If a friend discloses abuse to you, it means they trust you. Listen to them, believe them, and let them know you are there for them. Learning that a friend is being abused can be emotionally tough on you as well. Your friend may ask you to keep the abuse a secret. This is a secret that it not safe to keep. Encourage your friend to seek help and share their secret with an adult who can help them stay safe. Offer to help your friend find someone to talk to. Look up phone numbers for support services or go with them to the police or a counselor.

Offering support to a friend is a wonderful thing.

Talking It Out

It can be helpful to go to a counselor, doctor, or **psychiatrist** to talk about the abuse. These professionals are trained to help with situations just like yours. Don't worry about what to say. They will talk with you about what they can do to help and will also ask you questions so they can get to know you better. It is important that you feel comfortable and tell them the things you feel uncomfortable with.

Talking about things will not make them magically better. In counseling, you talk about very private and hurtful things. It can be hard, especially at first because you might have been keeping the hurt secret for so long that it is hard to let it out. The goal of counseling is to help you deal with and understand what has happened to you. Over time, the counselor will help you with your feelings and provide you with a safe place where you can talk about the abuse. Studies show that talking about the abuse can help people who have been abused cope with things.

Counselors can listen to you and help you.

How to Share

Telling someone about abuse can be very difficult. You may have tried to do it before but backed out because you did not feel comfortable. It can be helpful to prepare yourself before you disclose. Here are some tips for sharing and for listening to someone who might want to disclose to you:

- Tell your friend or a trusted adult that you want to talk in private about something that is very important.

- Tell them in as many words as you can that someone has been hurting you.

- If the person you disclose to is a trusted adult, they might be required by law to report your abuse. This will not get you into trouble. The goal of reporting is to ensure that you are safe. The abuse is never your fault.

- If you have told someone and they don't believe you, do not let this stop you from telling someone else. Some people may be shocked by what you say and they may not know how to deal with it.

If someone has disclosed to you:

- Listen and be supportive. Disclosing abuse is very hard to do and they may be frightened about what may happen next. They may not be able to tell their full story all at once.

- Offer them help. Do not tell them that everything will be alright. Assure them that you will be there for them.

- Help them find support. This will mean telling child-protection authorities or the police. Stay with them if they need to talk to the police or other authorities.

Chapter 7
Coping Toolbox

If you are being abused there are some important things you can do to help keep yourself safe. There are clues your body gives you to help recognize that you do not feel safe. Your stomach may hurt or have butterflies in it. You may be anxious about your surroundings or not be able to sleep. Other clues may come from past events. If you know that your parents become angry and violent when they drink alcohol, think about how you can stay safe the next time they drink.

Caring for Yourself

Taking care of yourself is an important part of staying safe. When you feel upset and frightened, it may help to take slow, deep breaths. Find a safe place and practice breathing deeply in and out of your nose. Writing about your feelings may also help you get through things. Write in a binder or a notebook and keep it in a private place. Make a list of the things you like about yourself. Understand that you are an important person and what is happening to you is wrong and not your fault. Abuse does not have to define who you are.

Safety Plan

A safety plan is something you can put together and follow when you are in danger or feel you may soon be in danger. Your safety plan can help you know what to do when you do not feel safe.

Here are some ideas:

- Write down where you can go if you feel unsafe (you can call this your safe place). This can be a room in your home, a friend's house, a public library, or a neighbor's house.

- Make a list of safe phone numbers you can call for help. Include emergency numbers such as 911, safe relative or friend numbers, your school, and free 1-800 helplines.

- If you are in immediate danger, phone the police or an emergency number. Leave the phone off the hook. The police may try to phone back if you hang up, which could anger your abuser and put you in danger.

- For very young children, know and write down your own address and phone number.

- Avoid being alone with your abuser as much as possible.

- On the computer, only share information with people you know such as friends and classmates. Do not agree to meet new friends you have only previously chatted with on the Internet.

- Understand that nothing you did caused the abuse.

Q: I have a neighbor who sometimes lets me stay at his house when my parents are fighting or kick me out of the house. He tries to hug me in a creepy way. Is it alright to let him do this if he is nice to me and gives me a place to stay?

A: If an adult is hugging you in a way that makes you uncomfortable, then it is not okay even if he is nice and gives you a place to stay. You do not have to trade affection, companionship, or sex for a place to sleep. It is not a fair trade and is exploitative. Your neighbor is an adult and knows this. Staying with him is dangerous. Try to think of other safe places to stay. Are there other reliable family members you can stay with or do you have a friend whose parents you can count on?

Q: My friend told me she is being physically abused, but she made me promise not to tell. Is this a promise I should break?

A: Your friend told you because she trusts you. The best thing you can do for your friend right now is to listen to her, support her, and encourage her to disclose to an adult who can help. If your friend does not want to tell, then this is a secret you need to break. Abuse is a safety concern, and it is important that your friend is safe.

Q: My mom is never home because she works all the time. Her boyfriend is supposed to look after us but locks us in a closet to go out drinking. I told my mom but she doesn't want to do anything about it. If I tell someone else, will I have to live in a foster home?

A: Although not all children who are being abused or neglected end up living in a foster home, it is a possibility. You deserve to be kept safe, which may mean your mom gets help to keep you safe. Whether you go into foster care depends on your experience with abuse, who the abuser is, and whether there are other places you can live.

Q: I told my friends that I was being sexually abused, and they did not believe me. What can I do now?

A: Sharing that you are being sexually abused is a very brave and scary thing to do, and unfortunately one risk of sharing is that you will not be believed. I am sorry that your friends did not believe you. This is hurtful and difficult to deal with. The best thing to do now is to tell a trusted adult. This is scary, considering what happened with your friends, but sharing it with an adult you trust is the best way to get the help you need. A trusted adult may be a teacher, counselor, or neighbor. It is their job to protect you and connect you with professionals who can help stop the sexual abuse.

Q: My dad is always after me to get good grades. He makes me feel like a failure, and he even calls me names like "idiot." How can I get my dad to see that I can't stand feeling like I am stupid?

A: Your father may think that he is only doing what is best for you. If you can, tell him that his words are hurtful and make it difficult for you to believe you can do well. Ask him to help you study instead of calling you names or ask a teacher or other trusted adult for help with school work.

Other Resources

Finding useful information about abuse can be difficult. You have to be very clever to find the kind of help you need. Librarians are not judgmental and can help you find books about abuse. Finding information on the Internet can be tricky. Some stuff is better suited for adults. Here are some trustworthy kid- and teen-friendly resources that can help you. The Web sites will contain useful information no matter which country you live in, but telephone numbers and referral services will be country-specific.

In the United States

ChildHelp: Help for Kids
www.childhelp.org/pages/help-for-kids
This site is dedicated to the prevention and treatment of child abuse. The Help for Kids section gives advice on how to protect yourself and how to get help. The organization also has a 1-800 hotline.

Kidshealth: Child Abuse
www.kidshealth.org/teen
Learn about child abuse, including what it is and why it happens, how to recognize it, and how to reach out for help.

Help for Kids: Emotional Abuse

www.helpforkids.bravehost.com

Find information and stories from other kids and teens struggling with emotional abuse and bullying.

The following hotlines can be used in the United States. If you are calling from another part of the world, feel free to call anyway as you may get a referral to another service in your region.

National Child Abuse Hotline
1-800-4-A-Child (1-800-422-4453)

National Victim Center
1-800-394-2255

In Canada
Mind Your Mind

www.mindyourmind.ca

This Canadian site is useful for teens and young adults everywhere. Read up on stress and mental health, and how to get help.

Kids Help Phone

www.kidshelpphone.ca
1-800-668-6868

This site has support forums for teens. Anonymous, confidential counseling is also available online and by phone (to callers in Canada).

Other Resources
The Hideout

www.thehideout.org.uk

This site is based in the United Kingdom and deals with domestic violence and child abuse. It provides information on staying safe. Handy hide-this-page and cover-your-tracks buttons allow you to access the site without others knowing and feel safe.

Glossary

abandoned To be left alone without support

addiction Something that is habit forming and very hard to quit

affection Physical expression of fond feelings or love

anxiety A feeling of worry or unease, also a disorder that makes a person feel excessive uneasiness, often leading to panic attacks

attachment disorder A disorder that makes it difficult to connect or make meaningful relationships

boundaries Limits or things that protect us

coercion To persuade someone to do something by using force or threats

corporal punishment Physical punishment

depression A disorder that makes a person feel low, tired, and hopeless

emotional disorders Medical conditions that affect how a person acts and feels

experiencing Undergoing; feeling

exploiting Using in a selfish or unfair way

gender The state of being male or female

human right A right that belongs to every person

humiliation Injury to someone's self-respect by making them feel ashamed and foolish

intentional Something done on purpose

isolating To cause someone to be alone or apart from others

manipulative Being selfishly in control of a person

perpetrators People who carry out a crime or a harmful action

poverty The state of being extremely poor

predators People who prey on others or exploit them

psychiatrist A medical doctor who specializes in the treatment of mental illness and disorders

psychologists People who study the human mind, emotions, and behavior

self-injury To deliberately hurt oneself through cutting or another method

siblings Brothers and sisters

switches Plant stems used to hit people with

traumatic Something that is emotionally disturbing

unintentional Accidental or not deliberate

violating To hurt or treat with disrespect

Index